Buster

And

Other Poems

Tripp Narup

*Our memories
are not ours alone.*

"You think dogs will not be in heaven? I tell you, they will be there long before any of us."

—*Robert Louis Stevenson*

Contents

Buster

And

Other Poems

Dog Poems

Buster

I killed my dog
as surely as if I had
stabbed him with a knife
or shot him with a gun.

Before we met
he had already felt the hand
of human kindness,
and the boot,
and the stick,
and the gun.

He flinched when I first reached to pet him.
He leapt to full defense mode
if surprised in sleep.

His paws *moved* when he slept.
I liked to think he was chasing rabbits
and not fleeing the man with the stick.

His was a fitful sleep
and I will never really know why,
despite dreaming beside him
for many years.

And then when he could no longer walk,
his joints frozen in pain,
I killed him — a coup de grâce,
a kindness of sorts.

But this I can tell you:
Death is never kind.
It may be quick, it may be painless,
but it is *not* kind.

There is no swift sword of grace.
There is just the hope
that just this once
when I played God,
that I got it right.

The Covenant

(Boomer)

We make a deal with a dog.
When we first take on the puppy,
we agree to play as often as possible.
We agree to let our fingers be nibbled.

We agree to be firm but fair
when explaining the strange rule
that you can't pee in the living room,
or anywhere else in the house.

We agree to throw the ball
even when we have tired of it.
We agree to be just as excited as you are
to celebrate the joy of coming home.

We agree to find you food that you like.
We agree to let you sleep on the bed.
We agree to rub your tummy and
especially we agree to take you on walks.

And in return, you agree to unbounded love.

We agree to take you to the vet when needed.
We agree to the expensive operation
even when we have our doubts.
And, oh yes, we still agree to take you on walks.

We agree to the pricey painkillers
that allow you to walk up the stairs.
We agree to not throw the ball
because you have grown too old.

We agree to a much shorter walk,
even though you want more,
you are panting and straining
and we know what you need is to go home.

We agree to help you up the stairs,
to grab you by the haunches and lift,
slowly making one stair at a time
back to your accustomed place.

We agree, when the times comes, to not let you suffer.
This is our version of unbounded love.
I have to wonder:
Who got the better end of the deal?

I have to wonder:
When my time comes,
who will grab me by the haunches as we climb
one painful step at a time toward heaven?

And in return, will I agree to unbounded love?

Phoning It In

(Boomer)

God knows, this is not what I meant
to happen, this was not my intention,
not my plan; I never wanted everything
to go so completely sideways.

I knew the moment the phone rang
that the news was bad,
that I would hate
what I was about to do.

I suspected that you were too old,
but I hoped you had one more in you,
one more time to play at doggie day camp
while I played elsewhere.

I was gone five days—one too many.
One less day and I would have made it home
to see you one last time, to say goodbye,
to tell you I love you (but you knew that already).

And so the phone rang. The message was short:
"Twisted gut, little hope of recovery,
do something in the next hour." Do something,
just do something, do something now, do something.

And so I phoned it in:
"Yes, doctor, put him down, put him to sleep."
And then I hung up and cried, knowing
that I had failed the simple task of being there.

Freedom

(Boomer & Buster)

I no longer have to hear the joyful barking
or see the enthusiastic jumping around
when I first pull into the driveway, knowing
you two have been waiting for the last hour.

No one inspects my packages, no one wants
a pat on the head or a scratch under the chin.
There is no one to answer the important questions:
"Are you my good boys? Are you my handsome boys?"

There is no one underfoot as I head upstairs,
Boomer hurrying to lead the way, looking back
to make sure I'm being herded correctly,
and Buster, following very closely at my heel.

There is no one who expects a bone
when I reach the kitchen. There is no quick exodus
to the living room carpet, where all bones
must be eaten according to some ancient canine rule.

No one sits next to me while I watch TV,
there is no chin on my knee, there are no ears
to scratch, there are no tummies to rub,
no balls to throw, no water bowls to fill.

No one guards the door while I sleep,
no one dozes next to my bed. I don't worry
about stepping on a dog when I get up at night.
No one barks at the boogey man at 4 a.m.

I have this strange freedom: No one depends on me.
I am free to travel, to visit friends and relatives.
I could be gone for months if I wanted,
but I just can't think of where to go.

9

Lessons

(Frisky)

I suspect our earliest memories never really fade.
I remember a tail, a wagging tail, a wonderful
delight of motion that clearly needed pulling.
I pulled your tail with enthusiasm ... and you bit me.

I still have the scar on my right pinky finger.
I remember being astounded at the incredible
redness of blood, being surprised at how quickly
my great game of pulling a tail turned bad.

It was just a nip, the kind a grown dog might give
to a misbehaving pup. It was the first of many lessons
I was to learn from my dog. You were a year younger
than I but clearly the wiser partner.

LESSON ONE: Don't yank on things that don't belong to you.
Particularly, don't yank on things that are attached
to someone else. It actually took me a long time to learn
this one. Not everything that wags needs attention.

Later, you taught me to stay out of traffic. You, a veteran
of chasing many cars and trucks, knew this was not for me.
You grabbed me by the diapers and pulled me back
anytime I might wander toward the road. My parents loved that.

LESSON TWO: Don't chase cars!
Don't chase things that can kill you.
Don't chase things that care nothing for you.
Don't chase the quick and glittery chrome.

When we moved to Florida, I learned more social lessons.
I learned to share. I would take a bite from the banana
and then you would take a bite from the banana.
We thought this was grand. My mother did not.

10

LESSON THREE: Share things with those you love.
Not everyone will approve, not everyone will understand,
but you will know what to share because it will bring you joy,
it will make you both smile (and, yes, dogs do smile).

Not all lessons went so smoothly. I remember watching you
pee on the palm tree in the front yard and like any male,
I thought that was a terrific idea. Why hadn't I thought of it?
The neighbors were not impressed and neither was my mom.

LESSON FOUR: Some people just don't understand
a really good idea when they see one. When that happens
you just have to pack your idea away for a better time.
Now I just pee on trees when I'm on a farm or in the woods.

When I was in second grade, you developed a tumor.
In those days, we didn't operate on dogs much.
You spent your last days hanging out in the shade.
You didn't complain, you didn't whine, you just calmly waited.

LESSON FIVE: Some things are beyond our control.
I never learned this lesson. I am not calm,
I am not accepting. Perhaps some day all my dogs
will get another crack at teaching such an unworthy pupil.

Party Girl

(Dora)

I.

I used to throw parties, I just didn't know
they were for you. But looking back on it,
it was you who thoroughly enjoyed all the people
who came, not me. You were the real host.

You clearly enjoyed wearing your lei
at the Hawaiian croquet party. And everyone
loved that we changed the rules to allow you
to chase the croquet balls and move them at will.

You were an expert at begging. My grandmother
always said "that dog has a square butt!"
You could sit up with your front paws extended
for as long as it took—everyone caved eventually.

But the one thing that always won them over
was the famous Dora Flop in which you
launched yourself backwards into the arms
of the unsuspecting, your tummy ready to be rubbed.

It was your favorite position: on your back
and on my lap, with your nose tucked under my chin,
content to have your tummy rubbed, content to snuggle,
content with life in that moment.

You were always the Belle of the Ball. Everyone loved you,
and you loved them as well. You entertained with your tricks
and begging, and your great joy in life
made us all want to go along for the ride.

II.
I remember the neighborhood kids with puppies
in a basket. At the time, I wanted a big dog,
perhaps a German Shepherd. I had my doubts about you.
You were small and unlike a shepherd, German or otherwise.

You had the markings of a Rottweiler, not a breed
that I ever really liked. I tried to resist, but clearly
the kids had their orders—the puppies had to go—
and I was an easy mark, I couldn't resist you from the start.

You were an adorable puppy … Adorable Dora!
I stole your name from a science fiction novel.
How was I to know that you would capture my heart
and I would mourn you forever, just like in the book.

I had already installed a doggie door, one sized
for a large dog. It was comical watching
your tiny little body poking through that great, big door.
If ever there was an aspirational door, that was it.

I kept looking at your paws and exhorting you to grow.
I wanted a *big* dog and your paws didn't promise much.
You turned out to be a perfect 30 pounds … not the big dog
I wanted but just right for launching yourself into my lap.

You were an awkward teenager—limbs too long,
hair not right, still chewing on everything and hell-bent
on jumping on everyone. But you grew up into a cute,
long-haired terrier who loved everyone—such a rare thing.

III.
There is one thing I never told anyone, not once,
but I will tell it now. Each night when we went to bed,
you required this one thing: You gently licked my eyelids.
I could protest or resist, but all for naught, you insisted.

You would lie on my chest, with complete confidence
that in this one thing, this one small thing, you would prevail.
It was a nightly ritual that I eventually came to appreciate.
Whatever might happen that day, I still received a gentle benediction.

I had a dream about you the other night. I dreamed
we were in a grocery store of all things and I had lost you.
I walked through the store and finally saw you making friends
(of course) with an old lady at the end of an aisle.

I called your name and you saw me. Your face
lit up with joy and you came bounding toward me,
and then you jumped straight into my arms
and we were so happy, just like we always were.

The Chair

(Dora)

When I turned 40, I bought myself a chair
for the living room. It is a black leather chair
with a footstool and a back that reclines.
It is a dad's chair, a captain's chair, a comfy chair.

It is the kind of chair that clearly belongs
to the owner of the house, the alpha male,
the one who pays the bills. It is a chair
that guests instinctively know is not theirs.

I had great plans of reading in my chair,
of conversing with friends from that chair,
of drinking wine and listening to music—
all from my magical, modern swiveling seat.

The moment it was delivered, you jumped
into my chair. The seat was exactly as wide
as your body. The padded arms were exactly
the right height to be your chin rest.

I could not have picked a more perfect chair
for my dog and you knew it. From that moment on,
it was "Dora's chair." You practically lived there.
I never once even thought of sitting in your chair.

And now, decades later—even two dogs later—
I still walk by your chair and am surprised
to not see you there looking up at me.
The chair is still here, empty and waiting.

Bodyguard

(Tuffy)

Even now, I'm not sure why
I needed so much protection.
I don't know why you were so adamant,
so fierce, so loyal, so dedicated.

You were always on duty.
No one could approach me
without a quick, sharp bark,
a warning, a clear shot across the bow.

If anyone moved to hug me
you barked, you growled.
I can't imagine what might have happened
had someone actually tried to harm me.

Perhaps that was the point all along—
just me knowing that I was safe,
that you were always looking out for me,
always protecting me, right there all the time.

You weren't alone in this trait.
My grandparents' dog, an otherwise
sleepy and pleasant basset hound,
often jumped in our car as we left.

He would sit next to me and growl and snap
at anyone who tried to remove him.
We would all have to get out of the car
so my grandfather could retrieve him.

You were both dogs doing your duty
as you saw it, as some strange canine god
had ordered, a duty that no human understood
except perhaps for me, in a wordless kind of way.

There was a time when my parents were out of town
and a babysitter was staying with us for the weekend.
I fell in a creek and bashed my head on a rock,
generating a huge knot on my forehead.

My sisters got me back to the house.
The babysitter tried to put ice on my head.
You launched yourself onto my chest
and dared the world to overcome you.

Such a brave woman—she plunked the ice
on my head, timidly saying "I'm not afraid of you!"
and promptly fled the room, very near tears.
And you stayed at my side, ever vigilant.

I was away at college when you died. You had attended
classes with my mother, content to sit under her chair.
You didn't bark, you didn't growl. Your bodyguard days
were over, your job was done for I was grown and gone.

Notes from the Loyal Opposition
(Gilligan)

We had the perfect life. We were the international
mixed doubles napping champions.
I curled myself into the back of your knee
and we slumbered with the best of them.

I brought you presents: mice, squirrels, and rabbits.
I dropped a huge water bug on your chest one night.
It was such a wonderful specimen and fun to bat around.
I was surprised when you screamed and flew out of bed.

You never seemed to appreciate my presents
but I never stopped trying. Sometimes I went for variety:
snakes, bugs, birds of all types. I always brought them in live;
you always chased them around and put them outside.

So why, after this fabulously successful partnership
did you find it necessary to bring a butt-sniffing dog
into our house? I cannot think of what I ever did
to deserve this snuffling, bumbling mess of a puppy.

She wants to *play* with me! She sticks her nose right in my face.
She chases me down the back stairs when I'm trying to make
a graceful exit to go hunting in the woods. I have had to insist
on you opening the front door so that I can maintain my dignity.

Worst of all, she interferes with my gifts. She runs over
and makes me drop my squirming prey but then she fails
to catch it! She lets it get away! I once spent days staring
at a bookcase, waiting for the rabbit that was hiding behind it.

I believe I made myself perfectly clear the day I climbed
onto your lap, climbed on top of the ever-present *dog*,
and settled myself right on top of her, at which point
I let loose a fart on her head that I had been saving all day.

I stood up, shook myself, looked you right in the eye
and made a dignified exit. My point was made.
I put up with *the dog* for the rest of my life—I don't whine,
I have my standards. But what were you thinking?

Doggie Porn

I have to admit,
I have been indulging
in doggie porn.

While at work,
I have been perusing
dog adoption sites.

I have been surfing the web,
admiring dogs in all their forms,
all their ages, all their sizes.

Each one is a possibility:
Bernie, the St. Bernard
with the unoriginal name.

He is big, but I bet
he would fit through
the doggie door.

Annie, the hound,
she looks so cheerful,
so photogenic.

She would like
the neighborhood kids,
she would play with them.

Ginger, the small,
sensible poodle,
only seven pounds.

Face it, small dogs
are easier, but I do like
the big ones.

Della, the black lab,
you know she is friendly,
you know she will sleep on the bed.

You know she will chase
the ball, bring it back
and beg for more.

And the names,
who came up
with these names?

Edith, Carlton, Levi
and Wyatt. Who names
a dog Wyatt? And why?

I want to find out.
I want to know Wyatt.
I want to know them all.

I want to throw the ball,
I want to take walks,
God, I want a dog.

Enough

A Galápagos tortoise lives to be over one hundred,
but a dog gets only 12, maybe 15 years.

Can you imagine playing fetch
with a tortoise? It might take decades.

And who really wants
a 900-pound tortoise on the bed?

The tortoise won't keep you warm,
it's cold-blooded (but not calculating.)

Tortoises don't sit up and beg,
they don't sit on your lap.

Forget about rubbing their tummies,
they *hate* being on their backs.

They don't bark or growl,
but they make funny noises when mating.

A Galápagos tortoise makes a poor pet—
lucky for them, they've got enough problems.

A dog, however, is the perfect pet:
loyal, playful, loving, and warm.

The "warm" part is especially important
on a cold winter's night, snuggled in bed.

Most dogs will play fetch
until your arm wears out.

Most dogs will sit on your lap,
lick your face, and beg for treats.

Tummy rubs are heaven for dogs.
We love to see them so happy.

So why do they get so few years?
They are so good at what they do.

Is it just a choice
between shell and fur?

Or is the dog's life so well lived
that a short time is enough?

Prey

(Boomer & Buster)

A fall day is perfect
for breaking out the crockpot.

Almost anything you dump in there
will turn out fine given enough time.

Oddly, this is a thing
that makes me miss my boys.

As soon as the crockpot
started to emit luscious odors
they stood guard in the kitchen.

They patiently waited,
their noses telling them all
they needed to know.

Chicken, beef, lamb, or pork,
they all required an honor guard.

There wasn't a single thing
cooked in a crockpot
that didn't require their presence.

I would try to get them to move,
I would try to get them to play.

They would not move,
they would not play.

The crockpot promised paradise,
and they would not budge.

A dog has patience,
he is willing to watch for hours.

His nose tells him that this time
it's beef, and there are potatoes.

He will ignore the potatoes,
he will ignore carrots and onions.

A dog knows in his heart
his job is to bring down the prey.

He may not be chasing the cow,
but he watches it,
slowly stewing in the pot.

My boys stalk the crockpot
with a hunter's instinct.

They know they will bring down
their prey, the cow is real to them.

And after hours of vigilance,
their faith is rewarded.

The cow has been brought to ground
and delivered to their bowl.

And who can say if everything
I have done was not at their bidding?

Who can say if they hadn't outsourced
the hunting to me? Clever boys.

The Cure

(Tuffy)

When you reached your middle age
(a mere eight years old or so)
you started losing your hair.

Your glorious, white coat
became a little tatty,
a little threadbare.

We took you to the vet
who said he had
a 100% reliable cure.

You needed to be "fixed,"
he said, and within weeks
your fluffy white coat would return.

As a young male, this seemed to me
to be a bit extreme. Surely there must be
another way, a different treatment?

The vet was adamant: this was
the only real cure, and he
guaranteed the results.

So, we had you "fixed" and your hair
regrew as promised. You spent the rest
of your days with a thick, white coat.

And now, some 50 years later
I examine my aging face in the mirror
each morning with some regret.

But as I note my ever-receding hairline,
I realize that thanks to you,
I don't really mind being bald.

Faith

(Dora)

When you were young,
we took a long walk
in the park every day.

You enjoyed smelling
all the new things
in the park.

You liked meeting the children,
who loved your long hair,
and sunny disposition.

At the end of our stroll,
we would come up the walk
next to the giant oaks.

One day, as we returned,
a squirrel fell out of the tree
right in front of you.

We were both startled.
A squirrel—what a gift
for a dog!

The squirrel made a quick recovery
and bolted off to another tree
while we stared, still stunned.

Every day, from then on
you stopped at that exact spot,
waiting for your squirrel.

Dear Dora, I would say,
a squirrel falls from heaven
maybe only once in a lifetime.

If you aren't ready for it,
it you pause, if you stumble,
it will likely get away.

You ignored my helpful advice,
you continued to stop each day
in full expectation of a heavenly gift.

Weren't you, after all, a good dog,
possibly the best ever?
Surely, God must know that.

You never gave up on God,
you daily gave Him a chance
to do the right thing.

Buddies

(Boomer)

I should have seen it coming.
After all, I got Buster to keep you company,
to keep you from barking at the world
while I was away during the day.

And it worked. Once you had Buster
to pal around with, you no longer
felt abandoned while I was at work,
you no longer barked at the world.

You insisted on being the "alpha male"
and Buster let you think so.
You always seemed to be intent
on keeping Buster in his place.

He could, of course, get you to do
whatever he wished. He was
(and forgive me for saying so)
the smarter of the two of you.

For twelve years, I enjoyed
coming home to your greetings.
You both headed outside at 3 p.m. sharp,
ready to deliver your barking chorus.

When I returned home, without Buster,
I knew it would change our lives,
but I thought you might enjoy
being the only dog for a while.

Within days, you were no longer waiting
in the yard when I returned home. Within weeks,
I would make it all the way up the steps
before you would awake from your nap.

I would jokingly tell people
that clearly Buster had been in charge
of the greeting committee,
but I suspected it was more than that.

I should have known
that after all those years of being pals
losing Buster would break your heart
just as much as it broke mine.

Other Poems

Decline and Fall

Your irises are all gone now, trampled
by the enthusiastic pounding of
dogs escaping the house and hoping to
take by surprise just one errant squirrel.

The dogs took the shortcut—over the wall
and through the iris bed—slowly killing
what I thought would be sturdy flowers, but
they proved susceptible to time and paws.

The exotic bulbs were just dilettantes.
The winters were too cold and the summers
too hot, April too wet, and August too dry.
These pampered plants were not meant to grow here.

The Japanese irises, the crazy
varieties of tulips, each one more
exuberant than the next, they slowly
gave way to the irresistible weeds.

The roses, well the roses never stood
a chance. I planted them for you, the one
with the patience, the sprays and powders, all
required to help these needy bushes thrive.

The hostas did well until one winter
when the city truck spread salt over them
like some Biblical punishment, killing
plants unto the seventh generation.

I had hope for the azaleas, which
bloomed when and how they should until they were
killed by vines that seemed to come from nowhere,
springing from the earth in just a day.

All that is left is the Rose of Sharon,
a plant that "thrives on neglect" according
to my gardening book. It has taken
over the yard, doubling its ranks each year.

In August, the Rose of Sharon erupts
in a cheerful plague of blooms that promise
new growth, renewal, and the hope of spring,
but I know damn well it is almost fall.

Lineage

The acorn does not fall very far from the tree,
which may explain the parade of frailties
passed on from father to son,
from father to son.

You smoked two packs a day until you died,
in no small measure from those cigarettes.
I smoked two packs a day for many, many years,
but I quit and they haven't killed me … yet.

You played piano by ear.
I use sheet music,
but I must admit that often the written notes
are more of a suggestion, a guideline.

You liked boats and planes, gadgets and gizmos.
So do I. I always have.
There is just no escaping this one, is there?
Of all the things I got from you, these I will accept.

You drank scotch,
poured it on your corn flakes.
I drank scotch but gave it up,
and I hate corn flakes.

You beat your wife and terrorized your kids.
You left them without a dime, without a word.
I have no wife, I have no kids.
I have dogs and I do not beat them.

The acorn does not fall very far from the tree,
but perhaps far enough.
I am a better man than you,
although not by much.

It is the scant space
between anger and action
that makes all the difference —
a space about the size of an acorn.

Living Memory

I. Death
It takes a long time to die;
we last much longer than we think.

Long after the terrifying fall down the mountain,
punctuated by a dull thud (full stop),
someone will remember
that your favorite color was green.

Someone will remember
that you liked vanilla ice cream
and that you meant to buy new hiking boots
but just ran out of time.

Long after the horrible realization
that the light you see really *is* the headlamp
of an oncoming train rushing to meet you,
someone will remember that you liked daisies.

Someone will say that your kitchen
had daisy wallpaper, your bathroom too.
Your bedroom had hand-painted daisies
on the walls, and the sheets were a daisy print.

Someone will remember that your car
had been stalling at inopportune moments
and that you meant to have it fixed
but just ran out of time.

Long after your beloved Dodge Charger
falls through the ice, the locals will remember
that you stopped to buy a six-pack of Michelob
which no one drinks there.

The locals will say that you were
passing through and wanted to drive
on a lake just once before you headed south.
And once, they will say, is all you got.

Long after your months of suffering
come to an end, your friends and family
will remember the jokes you told,
laughing in the face of cancer.

They will remember but not mention
that affair with a younger woman
and the remarkable fact that you
cheated on your taxes and got away with it.

Your friends will remember
that you lasted a whole year,
six months longer than expected,
as if somehow you had not run out of time.

It takes time to die, but time does runs out.
It takes five generations, sometimes less.

II. Memory
Your grandchild will remember
that you bought her a plush pony
for her fifth birthday, but her grandchild
will never know you, not even your name.

There is nothing in the genealogy book
that indicates you had a sense of humor,
that you had the patience of Job,
or that you liked to swim in the nude.

Your children will remember your face,
your various kindnesses and your
infrequent transgressions against them.
You do, in fact, live on through your kids.

The fifth generation is when
you really die, when it all ends.
They may hear stories about you,
but not one will have ever held your hand.

The fifth generation did not taste your pie,
did not learn your secret fishing spot,
and did not ever see you laugh or cry.
You are just a story to them, nothing more.

There are some who think you can live on
through your art or your accomplishments,
but does anyone know what Beethoven
ate for breakfast or Picasso for lunch?

There is just so much time allotted to us,
those few generations and nothing more,
unless you believe in heaven, in which case
you have all the time you choose to imagine.

The Political Poem
I Tried Not to Write

We will not go out with a bang.
We will not go out with a whimper.
There is no rough beast slouching toward
Bethlehem or any other damned place.

There is no tiger burning bright.
There is no center to hold.
We have no captain of our soul. We have
lost our way in the noisy wilderness.

What we have here is a failure
to communicate, a longing
for simpler times—Rosebud—
and the belief that God loves us.

This is how the world ends: with the
incessant din of self-righteous,
sanctimonious prattle—a sure sign
of the end of days, the end of mind.

Old Man

When I was only four or five years old
my sisters would always call me "old man"
because I was such a serious child.

I saved my allowance for a rainy day,
not knowing what that was. The coins rustling
in my piggy bank made me feel safe.

I used words that were too big. I seriously
believed in right and wrong and was confident
that I knew exactly which was which.

Now I *am* an old man and my body
has caught up with my personality,
I am now the man I was meant to be.

I am no longer so sure of right or wrong,
God or devil. I know of just these things:
my plants, my pets, and a few good books.

To all those who said I was too morose,
too studious, or too crabby, I have
just this to say: "Get the hell off my lawn!"

Questions for Galahad

Oh Galahad, perhaps I watched too many musicals
in my impressionable youth. How did I not notice
that a knight in shining armor does not save the day
but instead is just the beginning of the problem?

How were we to know that the best thing about you
was your horse, the one you saved from the drudgery
of the plow, the noble horse who thundered across the field
of battle, knowing they were in fact aiming for you?

Oh Galahad, was it really necessary to rescue
those damsels in distress? Perhaps they were
not so distressed but were hoping to plan
a wedding, with Galahad as the groom?

How were we to know where your heart truly lay?
You left so many women behind in your quest
but somehow there was always a stable boy
close at hand to attend your every need.

Oh Galahad, and what were you thinking
when you chose your moment to die?
Did you really expect anyone to believe
the mere sight of Joseph was enough for you?

After all your gallivanting, you swaggering knight,
were the battles and the blood and the damsels
and the derring-do all really just a way for you
to avoid bringing home the milk after work?

Death as a Young Man

Young man, with your casual saunter,
your easy, winning ways,
and your confidence
right down to your balls.

Young man, with your perfect teeth
and dimpled chin, I can feel the heat of you
even from here. Have you come for my pride
or my purse? Or something worse?

I have killed better men than you.
I have shot them in the streets,
I have destroyed them in firefights
halfway around the world.

I have spent their lives with abandon.
I have ground their souls to dust
from my corner office. I have sentenced
them to life in a cubicle with no hope of parole.

I have vanquished.
I have triumphed.
I have …
I have …

I have forgotten. I have forgotten how to win.
I have lain on my back and exposed
my soft, fat belly to your knives.
I have pissed myself in submission.

Go ahead, take it all. Take what you came for.
Just leave me this one year,
this month, this day,
this

Refuge

When I was young we hid beneath our desks
playing duck and cover, duck and cover.
Our teachers told us we would be safe
from the missiles in Cuba just miles away.

Our neighbors had a bomb shelter
where we played duck and cover, duck and cover.
It was stocked with food to last for months
and my friend Stevie said it would keep us safe.

The big buildings downtown had Fallout Shelters,
a new place to play duck and cover, duck and cover.
When the air and water became poison
the Fallout Shelters might keep us safe.

We learned in high school the strange comforts
of "mutually assured destruction,"
which did not seem as helpful
as duck and cover, duck and cover.

It was Little Boy and Fat Man
that had won the war and kept us safe.
It was Honest John the rocket
that kept the commies at bay.

The Minuteman, the Atlas, the Titan
and the Peacekeeper—all took their turns
standing guard to keep us safe.
We do not even talk about them anymore.

Sometimes I still want to hide under my desk
and play duck and cover, duck and cover.
I miss the notion that somewhere in the world
there is a small place that will keep us safe.

Babbage

There was a time when we just about had it
all figured out. You sir, Mr. Babbage, were
so close. Another pinion gear or perhaps
a fancier punch card might have done the trick.

We almost created that Victorian
ideal: every atom in its place willing
to perform its proper function according
to the grand design captured in your Engine.

There would have been nothing beyond the scope of
your marching punch cards, tackling even the most
difficult of questions and — who knows? — maybe
even peering into the strange human heart.

But we will never know, for Science has gone
mad. There are quarks, some of which are charming and
they spin! — like some silly music box with a
dancer perpetually *en pointe,* rotating.

It gets worse: There are leptons, gluons, photons,
bosons (of two types as if one weren't enough)
and—God help us—a Higgs, whatever that is.
How is one to wrap a gear around all that?

It is with great reluctance that I must beg
to inform you, Mr. Babbage, that the world
is a messy place, undeserving of your
attention and your incredible insight.

It is bad enough that we have particles
of a fanciful nature, but now they have
even cast doubt upon light itself. They have
invented a quantum—neither fish nor fowl.

What kind of world allows something so basic
as light to behave in such a capricious
manner? It is a wave when it chooses and
a particle when the mood strikes. What folly!

I must take my leave of you, Mr. Babbage,
your Engine has failed and so have I. There is
nothing in this random world that makes sense to
me, there is no order that I may cling to.

I must cast myself out into the stinking,
milling masses if I hope to understand
the vagaries of the human heart, none of
which fit in your Analytical Engine.

Tick

There is a time when fall
is just another season,
part of an orderly progression.

Like some great clock,
the seasons measure out
the Earth's simple habits.

At 20, we know what to make of it:
leaves will turn, there will be wonderful
clear, cool days, and then winter.

And that is all we know:
another spin of the wheel,
another change of clothes.

At 20, we have not yet seen
the Rose of Sharon bloom
a month early for no good reason.

We have not yet seen the year
when we can't walk across the yard
without skating on acorns.

We have not yet seen the year
when oak trees are barren
and there's not an acorn to be had.

We have not yet seen the year
of too much rain, or too little,
of bumper crops, or famine.

At 20, fall is any easy thing,
a predictable thing.
It is not a personal thing.

There is a time when fall
reminds us that life is short,
that there is work to be done.

Like some great clock,
fall is counting down now,
each year is one less to enjoy.

At 60, we despair.
We do not know
what to make of it.

We wake up one morning
and realize there might be
only a handful of seasons left.

At 60, we have seen
how cruel fall can be,
the death amongst the beauty.

We no longer assume
the river will not flood,
or the forest will not burn.

We no longer assume our knees
will work, our job will last,
or our dear friends will remain.

We no longer assume
the simple act of being here
will be enough.

At 60, fall is a personal thing—
we understand at last
this might be the only one.

Tock

No talisman, no trinket
will save you now.

Your prayers, your entreaties,
your incantations fall unnoticed
amongst the detritus of your life.

The room is empty
except for the clutter
of failure on the floor.

With every step you take
your feet rustle against
the flimsy attempts,
the botched efforts.

You are alone
with the timeline
of your creations.

There is nothing in this room
except what you have made.

You cannot bear
to look at the floor.
You cannot bear to move.

In desperation,
you cast your eyes upward,
toward a vague light.

Is there, perhaps,
a noble thought
floating above you?

Is there a happy memory,
a loving embrace or a kind word
just above your reach?

Will you float
or will you shuffle?

Fading
(for Bill)

As I sit here, I can see myself fading,
fading from your memory,
fading from your life.

I can tell you no longer remember
the float trip down the Meramec—
me paddling, you in your life jacket.

A true and remarkable friend
is one who braves a river
despite not being able to swim.

I can tell you no longer remember
the stone castle, the horseback ride
or the late nights we talked in the dark.

There were so many things we did.
I am not sure I remember them all myself
so why should I expect it of you?

I can tell you no longer remember
when the kids set off the bottle rockets
that chased us all over the yard.

I know the kids, now adults,
remember the year you had them read
the entire Constitution on the 4th of July.

I can tell you no longer remember
the comical groans for the 18th amendment
(Prohibition) and the cheers for the 21st.

As I sit here, I can see all the things
you have forgotten, but I am grateful
you still remember this: We are friends.

Dimensions

I have a tablecloth
my mother bought me.

It is a batik design—
something that involves
dye, wax, water and magic.

It fits my table perfectly.
The pattern seems designed
just for me.

I know for a fact
she never measured
my table.

I know the color
is an exact match
to her big, blue bottle.

The blue, hand-blown
glass is all that remains
of some beach in Florida.

The bottle, the waves,
the man, the memories,
are all on my table.

Things I know nothing about
murmur like small waves
breaking on the evening sand.

Persimmons

I have six persimmon trees in my yard.
Every fall I feel guilty for having used
none of the fruit, not a single one.

Even the squirrels avoid them
and they eat practically anything,
but they prefer my almost-ripe tomatoes.

It's just that persimmons are
so damned persnickety.
I wonder if that's the source of the word.

Could Darwin possibly be right
about this thoughtless fruit?
Does it really have some sort of advantage?

The persimmon has a reasonable taste,
it would make a good jam perhaps
or maybe even a tart.

But your timing has to be perfect.
Only an exactly ripe persimmon
is edible, the rest are bitter.

Bitter doesn't do them justice.
They make your entire face
screw up into a pout of dismay.

You can't believe anything
could taste like that.
And the taste won't go away!

Worse, it takes only one
not-quite-ripe persimmon
to ruin the entire batch.

The bitterness knows no bounds.
Just one disappointed fruit
takes its vengeance on all.

Blue Bomber

Driving is the simplest thing
and such a joy.

I learned to drive when I was 13
in a venerable 1959 blue Chevy pickup.

It was a four-on-the-floor
truck with a granny gear.

Predictably, we called it
the "Blue Bomber."

I loved it.

I can close my eyes and feel
the stick shift as I put it into first gear.

I can feel the clutch engaging
and the truck moving forward.

I can hear the door creaking
when it opened or closed.

I can hear the myriad rattles
and thunks it made as I drove.

It was heaven
for a 13-year-old boy.

Perhaps that old truck
is why I still enjoy driving today.

I love speeding down a winding road,
feeling at one with the car.

It's easy to understand such a thing.

It's hard to understand
the strange new job for trucks.

Even the truck itself must cringe
at being made to run down
people on a sidewalk.

I would like to think
that the Blue Bomber would refuse such a mission,
that pieces of transmission would fly about the road,
that the engine would seize, the tires go flat,
and the radiator explode.

A 1959 Chevy pickup
knew what was honest work
and what was not.

Catastrophe

The lake was gone long before I got there.
In the 1920s, it was a posh retreat
for the not-quite-wealthy.

They built charming lake cottages
along roads named Lakeview and Spring,
all surrounding the lovely Crystal Lake.

The cottages all had a front porch,
the better for viewing the lake
on a peaceful evening.

How I wished I could have seen it!
Like Ozymandias lying in pieces,
so the lake lay in ruins.

Sometime in the '20s or '30s
the dam broke, a forest grew
and what remained was … paradise!

The woods were thick with trees
that to a child seemed to herald
from the dawn of time.

Huge oaks, walnuts, maples, and firs
all competed for their slice
of this wooded heaven.

The lake had become a forest,
but the cottage owners still had
a pleasant view of an evening.

Imagine being a boy who lived
only half a block from Sherwood Forest,
a place full of wonder and mystery.

There were paths leading through the forest
to the heart of it all—the remains of the dam,
frozen in an instant of time.

Great slabs of concrete were broken
and twisted, only the sides of the dam
remained imbedded deep in the dirt.

The center of the dam was missing
as if God himself had punched a hole in it,
leaving behind only jagged shards.

As kids, we found this catastrophe intriguing:
What if you were in a boat when it happened?
What if you were on the concrete dock that collapsed?

What if you were downstream
and suddenly saw a wall of water
rushing toward you?

We loved to spin out the possibilities,
we could talk about it for hours.
It was the event we longed to have seen.

A wonderful spring-fed creek
ran through the middle of the dam,
pretending to be innocent.

But if you followed the creek downstream
you had to jump from one giant slab
to the next, for a very long way.

It didn't seem possible that mere water
could carry huge blocks of concrete
for such a distance.

When I was in junior high school
someone sold the forest to a developer
for high-end houses.

The lake, once again, was to be home
to the not-quite-wealthy,
but this time minus the view.

Bulldozers proved greater than
the force of water, making short work
of the remains of the dam.

They pushed over the trees,
they buried the paths, and then
they built houses … on top of springs.

It went well for a while,
all that dirt being moved around
put a cap on the springs for a time.

They built streets, they built houses,
people bought them, moved in
and started their new lives.

The first spring to escape was located
right under the old concrete dock;
it blew a section of curb high into the air.

A homeowner on a small hill
thought himself safe, only to come home
to a basement completely full of water.

The many springs took their vengeance
as best they could, but bulldozers, concrete,
pumps, and drains eventually tamed them.

In the end, the wonderful spring-fed creek
became a concrete canal with occasional
inlets for the springs to be allowed to flow.

Now, the cottages look upon … nothing.
The homeowners below have built
privacy fences, completely blocking the view.

You can't see their yards, or their windows.
You can't see the forest, the dam or the lake.
I feel like a door has been slammed shut.

If you drive down their street
into the old lakebed, you might
be able to see a glimpse of the old creek.

It is still encased in concrete,
but I have seen the hand of God before,
and in my mind I see His fist smashing it all to bits.

The Twins

They stand like sentries
guarding the front of my house.

For 100 years, they have grown,
they have sheltered, they have prospered.

It is unusual for two giant oaks
to grow to such a size, a mere six feet apart.

I call them the twins.
They are *almost* identical.

They are 90 feet tall or better.
I can't reach my arms around them.

For the 20 years I've been here,
they have protected my house and me.

All of my neighbors had hail damage,
but the twins would have none of it.

Like all twins, you *can* tell them apart
if you know them well, if you know what to look for.

My twins are easy to tell apart:
one of them is evil.

I don't say that lightly, I've had many years
to reluctantly come to that conclusion.

Let's start with the obvious:
the evil twin leans toward my house.

It is only his force of will that keeps
his trunk upright and not plunging through my roof.

He's been buckling my sidewalk for years.
His roots apparently resent my passing by.

One year, he dropped a squirrel
right in front of my dog as we returned from a walk.

She spent the next *decade* expecting another.
What a cruel joke to play on a dog!

But the worst thing he has done,
the thing beyond the pale, is … the squirrels.

For 20 years, two damned decades,
this tree has willingly housed squirrels.

Not just normal squirrels, oh no!
These are the world's dumbest squirrels.

They were apparently bred
for one purpose only: just to annoy me.

Every year, generation after generation,
they build a nest directly over my sidewalk.

They ignore millions of years
of squirrel evolution and improvement.

They ignore the obvious example
of their peers who build high in the tree.

These stupid squirrels, build their stupid nest
on a large limb that juts 90 degrees from the trunk.

The slightest wind dumps their stupid nest
and their stupid progeny on my sidewalk.

A dozen times a year, I clean up the nest
that lies on my buckled sidewalk.

I have to admit, it was with a certain amount
of animus that I had the large limb cut off.

It did no good. The squirrels
moved just one limb higher.

I can hear the evil twin snickering
as I clean it up, don't tell me I can't.

And late at night, as I contemplate
the longevity of an oak, and mine as well,

as I listen to the storm raging,
the wind assailing my twins,

I know that when the evil twin
decides to go, when he's had enough,

that he will fall, as he always intended,
directly, soundly, and finally right on my bed.

Luddites

What if the Luddites were right?
Maybe we should all be throwing
our shoes into the gears of life.

Is it too late to stop it all?
Can we pull the plug
on artificial intelligence?

Can we throw the robot
off the assembly line
just to save someone's job?

Which parts do we get to keep?
Does my heart medicine stay or go?
And what about the microwave?

Do I have to cook?
Do I have to sew?
Do I have to grow vegetables?

What does it mean to be a man?
Do we even know anymore?
Which parts of me are real?

Do we understand a single bit
of the great machinery
that molds us and spits us out?

Shrimp

There's a lot to be said
for yearly traditions—
they get things done.

For some, it's the annual
Christmas newsletter,
it keeps a family connected.

I have a Shrimp Party,
a tradition that dates back
to my grandparents.

Once they were gone,
I couldn't stand the idea
of losing the Shrimp Party.

So I turned it from
a family tradition
into a party for my colleagues.

The party requires so many things
to be done that might otherwise
languish on the To-Do list.

I give the piano a good dusting.
I mop and polish the floors.
I wash my grandmother's dishes.

I polish the silverware and
the silver serving bowl.
I iron my mother's tablecloth.

I hang the intricate stockings
my mother made, four of them,
on either side of the piano.

I practice the Christmas carols
we will sing after dinner,
our voices improved by wine.

I buy the shrimp:
eight pounds of farm raised,
two pounds of lovely wild peelers.

I throw out the old horseradish
and spice up the cocktail sauce
with the fresh, high-test, new jar.

And finally, I clean my grandmother's
crystal salt and pepper shakers,
a surprisingly tedious task.

The time it takes to remove
the pepper residue is time spent
reflecting on my grandparents.

There are always things
that need to be done.
Remembrance is one of them.

Embraer

The air is perfectly still.
The cabin is dark and quiet.
We sail through the night
as if time and distance were one.

The lights of cities appear from nowhere
and at times seem to climb right into the sky
as if they had been cut loose, freed
from the demands of gravity.

I am soaring through the night
toward my home in stillness
and anticipation. Soon I will be back
in the noisy world, my feet firmly on the ground.

But when I reach my home,
my quiet home, my empty home,
I will still be silently sailing through time,
just not through space.

My Dogs
(and cat)

Frisky
1957–1964

Tuffy
1964–1976

Droopy
(My grandparent's dog, circa 1965)

Gilligan
1988–2000

Dora

1993–2005

Boomer

2005–2017

Buster

?–2017

Acknowledgements

The poem "Buster" first appeared in *The American Journal of Poetry* , July 1, 2017.
http://www.theamericanjournalofpoetry.com/

The image on page three ("Dog Poems") is a photograph of a sculpture by Steve Jones.
http://www.stevejones-art.com/

Thanks to my friend and colleague (and poet) Kirk Swearingen who patiently tried to steer me in the right direction. I will always appreciate "The Side Bet."

Thanks to my friend (and author) Pat Piety who read my manuscript on short notice and offered helpful advice.

Typography

I was a typesetter for 10 years and still have an affinity for typefaces and their designers. There was a time when I could tell the difference between Century Schoolbook, Century Oldstyle, or ITC Century at a glance. I can't do that anymore.

I learned to love Optima and Palatino before they became part of the ubiquitous PostScript font package.

I chose Optima for the heads because I still think it's the most elegant of the sans serif fonts ... and it's a bit of a rebel. If you look closely, there's the slightest hint of an incipient serif—pretty cheeky for a sans serif.

I chose Palatino for the text because ... I'm in love with the capital "P." There, I said it. What's not to love?

P

Optima and Palatino are both the creations of Herman Zapf. Optima was released in 1958, Palatino was released in 1949.

Sometimes I still dream about setting type.